Separate Objects:
Selected Poems

Dennis Barone

Left Hand Books

Grateful acknowledgement is made to the editors and publishers who first printed these poems. Magazines: *Abacus, Confrontation, Figs, Generator, Giants Play Well in the Drizzle, House Organ, Juxta, Lyric &, O.ARS, Pivot, 6ix, Some Other Magazine, Talisman, Texture, Tight, Washington Review, WRLD WR 4.* Chapbooks and Limited Editions: *The House of Land* (Spectacular Diseases, 1986), *The Territory of Innocence* (Writers Forum, 1987), *Unfold The Mid-Point Now* (Open Township, 1988), *Questions' Purpose* (Writers Forum, 1992), *New.ark* (Potes & Poets, 1993), *Hard Fallen Bony Lapse* (Texture, 1996). Anthologies: *How The Net Is Gripped: A Selection of Contemporary American Poetry*, eds. Rupert Loydell and David Miller (Stride, 1992), *The Gertrude Stein Awards in Innovative American Poetry, 1994-1995*, ed. Douglas Messerli (Sun & Moon, 1996). Books: *Forms / Froms* (Potes & Poets, 1988), *Waves of Ice, Waves of Rumor* (Zasterle, 1993).

The publisher wishes to thank the John W. and Clara C. Higgins Foundation for funding this book and the Dutchess County Council on the Arts for technical assistance.

Cover: *Trackings IV* by Marilyn Stablein. Mixed media on paper. Pine needles, bark, ashes and mud.

Left Hand Books website: http://www.lefthandbooks.com/lhb

Designed by Bryan McHugh.

ISBN 1-880516-26-8

Manufactured in the United States of America.

Contents

Separate Objects

Touring

The men who set up the barricade
shot the grower and took the money.
People still talk about it.

The fog

one must
re-
search (not read)
to write

the poem
these days

"it takes
           about 180 hours

to enter the data in a computer
for a single stride"

1896- Walter Elmer Schofield bicycled
across northern Europe with William
Glackens and Robert Henri.

Geography

To tell the reader what's held inside.
To say where this place is that the speaker lingers.
To say what is incomplete, lost; what mattered so.
To say why the speaker doesn't live up to expectations
and why the speaker fails to say what's necessary.
To say where the door is and of what it's made.
To reverse touch and sight: literally / figuratively.
To be inside, to be outside.
To be here, there, and everywhere.

The Human Condition

Outside in the woods you will go to play again. Outside beneath all that water, outside beneath the ice and the branches you will hold your breath and count. You will play with fire. Outside you will feel the need and speak it and not mince words. Outside you will have no need to sit down, to be calm, to whisper after the harangue and the questions that even the brave lion wouldn't ask. Outside there is no one left and there are no words, no neighbors, no tears, no capture. Outside in this still weather you might feel purged, might even feel sanctified; revealed on the stand before the branches crush your fabled roof.

Adages

Age
Time is an abstract subject but it can be expressed in very specific poetic ways; hence, we speak of the "hands" of a clock. You cannot wrestle with these hands nor even shake them.

Wisdom
Learning to build a fire from sticks can be frustrating if one knows about matches. The sparks turn into flames.

Art
Once I was part of someone's photography project. In it I was a clown. The dog looks one way; I look the other. At the end the poem turns to God.

Religion
Mrs. Peck, Chairwoman of the Church Decorating Committee, succeeded in her goal of providing floral decorations for the Church's Easter service. Throughout her ordeal, she managed to keep up her housekeeping duties in exemplary fashion.

Biography
The "pear" became an "ear" and the "p" became the letter with which he wrote 111,158 poems.

Popular Music
"Sunny," "Brandy," "Wendy"—why is it that when we're young there's a song for everyone we know?

Give Back To Things Their True Names

Begin with the word tradewind but end with the word storm. Hands all slippers, berate the poem by not including the poet. The mind's baffling encounter with objects says that all high hats did not get knocked off (this time) nor were all embraces returned. For the poet the only hope is to reply to the image with another: rabbits displayed on Chanticleer plates, for example. It is at this point that consciousness always gives rise to the poem! Orreries blushing orange in perfected circles of rust, for example. Or, chairs stacked along chained isles, etc. Yet, the black ribbed guests still exchange their gloves. It is not a pretty sight. It is a sad one. In the nutshop all missiles are erect while in the distance is what's left of our legs. Further in the distance is a solitary self that is no longer able to detach itself from the objects it perceives. Give back to this mute self many splendid suns or one and a light by which a true name is seen so that it can begin again, so that it can sound the all-clear again, so that it can open for business soon.

Elegy

Shoe
Black shoe that has no path
and the no path that has no color
lead back to the start of school.

Red
This is the sweater that cheers us on
to the game and after the game we return
with our gloves to the parking lot on Woodrow.

Twin Towers
In the voids of the towers there are the wings
that extenuate vision. These are the lines
that you dedicate to the poet Wallace Stevens.

Firs
Why is it that they point upwards while if you
lean back in the chair you'll fall down?
This is all that you know of the most advanced science.

Empty
This is the saddest part of all.
The Buddha cannot fill these voids.
The reader cannot read these lines.

Travel
There is no getting away from it: not
the red of the sweater, not the voids in the towers,
not the hands of the clock nor those that greet you
in the morning.

The Night Sky

It boxes me in this room, knocks me down
to planet earth. If I get up again, will
you be there to greet me? Will you return?

Free Financial Aid

Free the Chicago Seven! Free the Panthers! Free
the beginning from the end! Free the left from the right!
Free the bread from the loaf! Free the Chicago Seven!

Child's Face

The child doesn't remember. What will you tell the child?
The child doesn't remember. Will you teach the child?
The child doesn't remember. Have you forgotten, too?

Footsteps

They lead nowhere. They are heard, but are not
seen. This is even sadder than all that came before.
They will never pass this way again.

Wake

Manipulation alone coordinates
commemoration for these soldiers.
Their testament lives on
spontaneity; it never
rots in the mud of national security
though the pols would like it to.

Individuals proliferate in every
marketplace while the soldier's camaraderie
thickens accounts with examples: one
war, many profits. That simple.

The enemy mimeographs combat;
the soldier churches disgrace
during all these hardly remembered
but difficult consistencies. What
character he has! the generals exclaim.
A truly modern hero.

Getting Down To Business

Go ahead, play the part of the Fool, but with genius. Herein whoop it up, then imagine faith—if you will. Let context comment for awhile on the speech acts of characters, on the hand that holds the phone. Descriptions get in the way in the same way that talking does. What's the big picture after all? The funny man from Fairfield said let me check my e-mail *before* we go to the e-bar. Don't say "love." We who obtain that glory are put down by those who don't. It was so like him to do so. It was so like her to have thought so. They know all of this. This year the trees fell off the leaves.

Sweet Chariot

Across a hostile desert, across a turbulent sea, the striped shirt is back. They still call you "Bones." Though good appearance only whispers your success, the echoes make pleasant listening. You wanted to be a musician, after all. The stripe is back, only it's narrower, fatigued by a hostile desert, become a thin peppermint stripe, at best. The stripe is back, a thin collar, too tight (who cares?), an instrument of torture. What happened to Jamina Iwanska's leg is now happening to your neck—but who cares? A tab or round collar with its own collar pin; the pin left in. You are caught in the hierarchy. No longer free to wear a baseball uniform. (Old Salt it was.) That is, memory, no longer uniform. It is single needle sleeving, the needle left in and free now to rip at your wrist. Oh, Mother. What is this? You want to hit home runs: the Kid you are called: *Bones.* You want French cuffs, fine fabric that is both Sanforized and mercerized. What is capitalized? You are confused. The stripe is back. You want to follow the railroad tracks like an Indian ear to the track, like Jack Kerouac. Where? *Dick Tracy* followed by *Art Linkletter* followed by *Mystery Theater* ("wouldn't miss this," "Case of the Missing Heads") followed by *Man Against Crime* with Ralph Bellamy and when Dad comes home will he chase you away to watch Paddy Young versus Ernie Durando? Will he chase you to bed saying, "The federal government should adopt a permanent system of price and wage controls"? You thought they knew what they were doing. So did Irving C. Freese who called the proposed all-purpose highway "exactly what the doctor ordered." The stripe is back. The solid color tie is basic with this shirt. So ends your last trip to bat: flied out somewhere over Korea Bay. Giacomo Rimini, an opera singer, died today. As one voice dies, so dies another: yours. Go forth and swing.

The Mentor

Roses, he said, not jonquils.
I took this to mean that
the poem had thorns as well as
blossoms.
Was it the blossoms or
the thorns that I removed?
He never spoke to me again.

In The Center Of All Things

The poet who writes
speaks from the center of
silence.
Silence is not darkness
but is a bright white light.
It is like the bright white
that surrounds the pupil
in the eye of the madman.
It is not the same.
It is not the same
because it is unnameable.
It is that property of
contrariness that seems
impossible.
Incarnate in the poem
it is magical.
Words are wings
on which we fly to meet
in the center of all things.
But how can silence be named?
And what is that bright white
that surrounds this ornament
I wish to speak?

Objects

Handheld

the notebook
as camera.

captures
not the world
but the thought

a record
a re / cording of
what
has preceded a
re / chording,
tuning
the instrument

the instrument scrapes
at the surface of language

a vessel
neither full nor sailing

object
emptied of all it held
waiting
to be read

Arise, Smooth As Flames

My
legs like wings
up high in the sky.
Beautiful robes
covered us in ash.
Shadows stroked
the wet underside
of our dreams.

The streets have
no names. The
names have no
parents. Set
free in the rain
they repeat
their beginning,
their beginning.
Set free in the rain
they repeat their
beginning.

Our flesh burns.
We breathe no
more the breath
that began
in the first
instance, in
the first syllable
of our names.

Separate Objects

A reflection of *construct*
as a state to be overcome,
obliterated!

Incapable of fulfillment,
short steps from identification
imitate.

The author edges the
seam. The irregular
pattern never written,
detonated.

Imagine:
we're fond of talk,
a precise norm
condemned.

Anticipation washed
beyond insistence
a symbol

that calls attention to
enterprise.

Apprenticeship
closes the last word
regarding difference

an abstract
circle no one
can name

a blind and
certain experience
of miracle.

Yellowed,
the affirmative idea:
to describe and
analyze.

Exact,
like everything.

The Objects Of Our Attention

On a mound
pine needle bed
turns red with
decay. Beneath,
sculptured rock
curved by
beating river mallet
of waves. Further
out two men
paddle between sight
and four tree island.
Is their line
caught in a tree?
Hawks leave a tree
flushed by shouts,
by pulling on the tree?
On a side path
a muskrat becomes
tomorrow's fossil
in today's mud.

Evoke senses!
Be done with stiletto knives
and lottery games that shine
on ad pages. What is
a body anyway?
Ecstasy.

Find an analogy in the natural
world: blue iris and a yellow
flower. "Yes, perfection
is not an accident." She
looked about the world and then
asked, "which way?"

"I don't know. My hands
are too soft to twist open an answer."

Bees swarm to their hive.
The spider knows its web.

Must I howl like an owl
or any of various nocturnal
creatures to make you see
those lines under your wrists,
those lines you call your veins,
they are the blue of a spider's web?

At night the flames were the winds
that calmed with your winks and
yet together we were warmth moving
toward flame.

"What direction?" you ask.
"I don't know.
My hands are too soft to twist
open an answer."

We've come to rock.
Hoe the soil and more rock.
These pale margins of night
are black bands suffused
with indications.

We move out of winter and night into
dawn, up through spring and early
morning to mid-summer and high noon.
When water is enough, we nonetheless
reach for a star.

Feel my heart!
To hear your foot upon the stair
—that star!

When I see your eyes,
how other than as a vision?
At night, the prayer said;
the skin, touched.

Cloaked, all lines cut,
free from tentacles that rip
being from self. The rock
sings: "I must not
invent myself anymore."
Cloaked, a single spirit
stretched toward a fusion
with the full moon.

It was morning, winter
mountains high above
the river. Cold hand,
that is obvious. What is
a person away from this place,
these hills, this whiteness?
The barn goes unpainted.
We go into the mountains to build
a fire. It was there,
we'd fall to any desire.

The granite was hard and in ridges.
The ceremonies were slow and tedious.
They were inside because of the rain.
It was hot, very hot.
The flesh left splinters; the others,
flowers.

I ask to be
baptized
west of nowhere
in skin soft folds
of I don't know
what: the rock.

The prayers of both cannot be answered.
We haven't seen when we thought we saw.
Vision—did we not ask of what use?
And of what use to ask?
This is the moment that might have been.
Even the stars take their lives
in one sudden blaze.
Cold hand, that is the break line.
Braced frame bore no reminder
of existence as trees.

Unmask my emblems.
Separate me from the world.
We were in the world—
once. Sure of it.
Reflective, not reflexive;
ordinary, not ordained.
And our house was
ordinary, too; not
ornamental, but practical.

How can I do
what the amoeba cannot:
substitute?
How can I speak,
if within is only silence?
Out of the silence,
a dinosaur on the page?

Pine needle bed turns red and

Wise, we were.
We knew words
were artifacts and
hewed them to our
liking. The two of us,
young. That first

morning we dove
into the river and
the river went suck.
No enemy then,
but the fog.

The foundation lies buried
beneath the skin. Mere
boundaries shimmer;
then fade. A recurrent
theme haunts. This sphere
is a glove. A car
through the phone booth and you
all that night trying to get
me on the line. Cold hand,
that is the break line.

Beyond reason; beyond memory
for a moment all turned
white again and there
in the textured folds of an opaque
stock we glimpsed ourselves
reading this and writing more,
together, yet kept separate
by the words we wrote.

And then we made up.
If it had not been this,
would it have been some other?
Objects of our attention
dismay us. If not a mirror,
some other reflection also
revealing blemishes.

Nightly. It was
the make-up mirror,
forgotten and believed to
have been lost. Argued

over, intensely. Oh,
but it was nothing.
Found, it regained its
somethingness, its "personal
value" once again.
Beyond reason, passion
turns all white and
there in textured folds of so
many rumpled sheets
we glimpsed ourselves
embracing.

At this precise moment
there is an egret out
at the end of the wash;
bunkers, too, but
further out. No gulls now,
but plenty of plankton,
enough for all:
bunkers, egrets, and gulls
too if they so choose.

Someone says it is
an American egret.
I have known them
as Snowies,
the smaller version of Greats.
The Eskimos have seven different
words for our one word "snow."
My neighbor and I have two
names for one egret.
The bird flies free from the wash,
out beyond the bunkers and their
attendant blues, out toward
the other side. We remain
where we are; the tide
ever flowing away from us.
Who knows?

Six hours from now
we might yet again be.

If not for the fact that
a tidal wave hits us:
our cups, our saucers,
feathers, and neighbors,
washing the bruise of work
away, salting our eyes,
and tanning our hides.

We cut the vine of our one body
and wrap ourselves around the embers
of an eternal bed.

It is odd that at this very
moment I look around and
take note of the various
shades of red in the bricks
in the walls that surround
me and for just a moment
I remember your dress.

What's Appropriate For A Pause

"no language is so
copious as to supply words
and phrases for every complex
idea"
James Madison

I think of my work as sculpture.
At least, while I'm writing it.

(inaccuracy is unavoidable)

I think of my work as music.
At least, when I've done writing it.

The shade is drawn.
The shade is still drawn.
I'm coming more and more to think of revision
as expansion.

Words are ideas.
There are some ideas that words cannot express.
Therefore, words are not ideas.

One fortune cookie with two fortunes
that said the same thing.

Something must happen
in order for something to be
anything.

How is poetry different from *writing*?
How is writing different from *poetry*?
(This is a rhymed couplet.)

No models not folded in mine:
definition by example—*disconcerting*
—*red ink showing through white out.*

"I'll write to you again in a week
or so with any further thoughts
I might have or just to let you
know that at that moment I didn't."

That would be a monument!
This, a moment opening to others.
Hyperbole: a lie that does not deceive.

Authority
is its own excuse for being—

Proto-Emersonian:

What a fine day this is!

And the Greek men of the Marathon
Restaurant have stopped dancing for the night.

(Antithesis.)

It's a secret of baffled Zen.
People in "uneducation" subtract rules.
It's a secret—to baffle Zen—essential—
in experience most process a secret.

What resumes after the time passes?
An umbrella, a hand, an open book.

"One would not read the book
unless one already understood
it," said one.
And the other:
"it's all genetic."

That his name is Jacob Johnson,
  his mother's name was Dorcus Simons.
That she was a white woman,
  at Accomack, in Virginia.
That Mr. Thomas Kirkly and Doctor Ridgely,
  in Kent and in Dover, know him.
That he labored in that country.

Tolerance Integrity Moderation Diligence
Justice Philanthropy Kindness Gentleness

Mercy

Self-help health

The fire that spirit stokes within
Prefer the traditional

Oblivious to the demands of fashion
Propel by continual self-doubt

Prefer the fashionable

Also Thomas Casbon, who saith he
  ran from Lee Master,
  at Little Pipe-Creek Furnace,
  Maryland.

grab express milestone success
take away one like day
born words report deeds (mis
tenacity laudable remember notable
beat raise sing praise
grab express milestone success
take away one like day

evoked moon named thing described
but what dream is too metaphor completely?

pretension photocopied each one not just
topical versus political Vietnam Apollo-man
word one word more than definition fragrance or law

What's appropriate for a pause?
The leopard has changed his stripes.

A toast use of the page or Black
Mountain etymology for the specific thing
named like the Pope, a phone number.

Is that a bad thing?
Will it get me stuck here
for life? Is that my
style? What is style?

My statement regarding your
question is a question and
not a statement. Question
is more important in my work:
more important than what?

I think of my work as sculpture.
At least, while I'm writing it.

I think of my work as music.
At least, when I've done writing it.

(Note: relation between parts is not
  necessarily the same thing as narrative.

Different notions create different sounds.
Or, should that be "different motions"?

Come on. Let it spin.

Is There More To A Line Than The Time It Takes To Say It?

Beads of water cling to the window pane. From where I sit looking in all directions could there be any other window, water, beads? Is there more to a line than the time it takes to say it? The line is now expanded not by breath, but by motion. There is the line that is an object and the line that is a vehicle for some unnamed and often disguised other. The first type is preferred and is to be trusted. I include in it two cylindrical objects: one contains salt and one contains pepper.

If this were not to be of beads, but of a continuous line pointing to an ever diminishing dot that could, in turn, be but one of the original beads, if this were of that line, could I, from where I sit, ever have framed this?

The poem then, as you can see, radiates toward infinite possible relations. As it radiates, the poem often questions those relations. For example, in the present (especially in the non-timeless present) is the poem an object? Is it water on window seen as beads on string felt? Is it only its perfect self as this of all things is most of all not that scene of language, but an imagined scene with window, water, beads; cylinders that contain and a seated intelligence that perceives a way in which they combine around lines as both lines and other?

How It All Washes Off

We talk too much. Do we not?
In all words there are other words.
And here is more talk:
the men of the Enlightenment owned slaves
and as soon as the young reporter
shows a little innovation the editor
tells him to strip down so that
the audience can understand. We
are slaves of convention. Is there
any escape from this circle of talk
enfolding upon itself endlessly?

I can swear that the other night I
dreamed a conversation with Samuel
Sewall and Duncan says,"Our
lines in poetry do not come into
line until we hear them."

The page is blank and white.
The road is long and black.
No two words are the cloak
that covers all thought. No
one word is the name:
the boundary extended,
no longer private land but
public. Do the best thing:
be the cartographer of categories.
Then will the bridge be burned?

Neither foreigner seized the weird
height of forfeit. The distinguished
family by virtue of their language
extended their source. Is it
toe the line t-o-e or tow
the line t-o-w? Iron resolution.

The observer carefully notes effects
of sense impressions and the
faculties set in motion by these
impressions. The observer then
tries to establish the same
operations in the mind of the auditor
by reporting the experience as
closely as possible to its original
but all the auditor hears is
Chilean music from the 1920s
based on the poetry of Li Po.

A finger disagreeably placed
—already—
so as to spoil the whole work,
a perfect work and a finger of blame
pointing.

I go back to "Little Gidding"
as to a place. It is a
poem that shakes me with
recall. A ruined world
and a place no longer
outside the poem, outside
the monument, outside the
moment: a perfect work,
a moment, a finger to spoil
the whole work that can
not cease but know the
whole place. Determine
that the thing can and shall
be done and find the way.
If the poem has any point
then this is point, shaft,
and bowstring. But how
move from spec to speculation
when there is no peace?
There is no peace

because there is no passion.

The distance between word and word
is pinioned to the chest.
Imagine a line with wings!
Spiritual entities must knock from within.
You must ask permission to leave.
The spirit of shadow is ash.
The attendant is no doorman.
Saint Jerome speaks from the wall.
Lava overwhelms the walls.
If chimneys burn stacks of volumes,
then the attic is a place of style.
Their tongues walk the earth.
The bodies riddle answers.
Their homes are arrows.
The streets are unpaved and once were.
The hydrants have no patents.
Rituals are brief and cogent.
Please identify.
Religion demands sacrifice.
The incense we burn is exhausted.
Our priests have no party interest
and are silent and silence
doesn't speak no matter what
the context. The government
we lived by has perished.
Mornings we shop in malls.
Mountains breed insects.
Level them and export the dirt
before it's stolen too.
Remove the flesh of words
from the bones they protect.
There is our house.

One day we waited for USDA
handouts of cheese and butter.
On the same street the next day

we waited to get a glimpse of a
movie star. This is the street
corner where the bad guys hang out
in his new movie. I suppose
that's a line. Can you
count on what you count on?
Prophet of ill: man and woman
infants still. There is a way
around the flame as well as
through it.

"The purpose of diplomacy is to prolong
a crisis." Recollection and anticipation
fill up almost all our moments. "Idiot,"
originally meant "private person."

And hence we have the word
"crescendo."

Body equals being; if your
weight goes down you are less.
We'll have to wait and see.
Does the spring at the old
spring house still spring?
"The Universe is all," Hobbes
said, "that which is not part of it
is nothing; and consequently no where."
Time is the enemy of our happiness
(summer ends), the ultimate enemy of our
happiness. I cannot remember
the last time we spoke.
Send a postcard if you wish.
Oh, yes. I'll use it for kindling.
This then must be the part called
"winter." There are no tracks
in the river, nor fish on the road.
The clock tells time, but the audience
is speechless.

When the subway reached my stop
I got off. I walked up to the
surface, the street and bought
a newspaper. It was a very hot,
sunny day. By the time I turned
the corner of my block my sweaty
palms were filled with newsprint.
Upon entering my house I read
my palm so to speak. There
were the names and events of the day.
I was surprised how easily it washed off.

There are only four or five ways
to understand this.
If you are sitting, are you also saying?
If you are saying, are you also thinking?
If you are thinking, are you also believing?
Ask the librarian for Erasmus
and you'll get an eraser.
Bliss Carmen, Richard Hovey, John
Vance Cheney, Robert Gilbert Walsh:
poets, c. 1910, liked by E. P.
Set fair for Roanoke.

My parents gave to the campaign to re-elect the president.
I tried to show them the rainbows in the sink and
motioned that the student council be abolished.
They were incredulous. Didn't we prove ourselves?
We lit up the night and lived like stars after all.
We picked at geography as well as correct opinion.
But the phone rang; the record, ended.
There remains no mark for the exclamation
that is also a question. At the end
philosophy will be based on neurological data.
A return to the original turns into what it is not.
Can you imagine the surprise? How brief it takes
to revert to the natural state. There is this page
that must be filled. What else is it here for?

We fancy that people are individuals, but so are pages
and every page goes through every point in page history.

The net of a continual present neither pardons
nor preserves. Shoddy with tricks,
images in eyes, paintings work a hard,
clear light. J. comes up the fourth
fairway. I join him. We play a few holes.
He sees something wrong with my chipping
and gives me a brief lesson. When I'm back
home in the late afternoon I'm a better man.
That night I turned on the light and began
to write: "I do not know for how long...".
Did you say structure or stretcher?
They found the body but the person had gone.
Any phenomenon of human behavior can be deciphered
like a language. Bring to each situation
what you need. Oscillations travel away
from the speaker at the speed of sound, so
when the word "so" is uttered the beginning
S sound is already 120 feet away
by the time the O sound begins. An
Iroquois speaker can smoke a pipe while
talking without any distortion of voice.

Does the surface disguise or show?
Phylogenetically, the ear is the most recently
acquired sensory receptor.

The manuscript reads:
de maligni Spiritus infestatione

"And I will add, *Man,* who is a *Sociable Creature,*
and should exhibit *Social Affections* by some
visible Tokens, is here furnished with *Tears*
for that purpose, beyond any other Animal."

Zonder Suiker

All of them.

Confused about the date,
the day that it was or
the day that it was becoming.
All of them. Always
looking for two if by land
or three if by sea.
Either way
the red that's in their eyes.
Fire.

Why does the word tart
refer to a sweet?
Why not, say, a rabbit?

Note: the Consulate can
secure every corner
but not shelter a single man.

"G" demonstrates
words' preciousness,
a gutteral sound—
each time as if it's
your last breath.

A lot of words
All of them from the outside
A fence
keeping us out
how few of them felt
as from the inside
how few
when there are none
those

such as these
referred to here
say nothing
but shape form and volume
there is nothing to drink
and we are thirsty

In a new speech
when she said
Jane Addams
everyone thought she said
John Adams.

"Democracy like any
other of the living faiths
of men, is so
essentially mystical
that it continually
demands new formulation."

I don't like to shout

across chasms

never mind

rooms.

You dressed a TV
ignoring your normal
vocabulary. Even the
word "cassettes" is
repeated for a second
time. You want the
practice to make
communication easy and
the equivalent of important
address. The words and

phrases will stamp you
as charming. Admire
buildings. Beg their
pardon by saying,
Pardon.

The outbreak. The intake.
The fumes. Not perfume.
The center. The periphery.
The correct. Not the false.
Sea gull. Car. Light.
Water. Brick. Cement.
Road. Street. Intersection.
Store. Window. Door.
Furniture. Bottles. Papers.
People. Ducks. Birds.
Tree. Roof. Sky. Plane.
Window. Smoke stack.
Blinds. Curtains. Shutters.
Steps. Lights. Desks.
Offices. Houses. Stores.
Windows. Doors. People.

"In Amsterdam,
the head has taken over
and the heart has
almost disappeared."

I thought you would
kiss my hand,
but instead you
scratched your nose.

Maybe smell is
the central fact
of who we are.

A week ago

we saw
Livingstone's
grave.

Stanley
was nowhere
to be
found. You

hear?

This word means
only one thing.
Nothing will be
allowed to mean
anything until
this word means
only one thing.

I have my doubts.
Few bricks.

The city cries out:
Come out! Come out!

We sit in in in
the house. Insistent
in our ways
against its. The city
cries; we plug up
our ears.

Our ears, our ears
—have wings.

A primary today

and a slogan

Don't Bite The Hand That Beats You

Re-Elect The President

and tomorrow

Remarkable flowers
lift themselves
up in the morning
in the sun
they sweat
and their smell is so
sweet

What a map!

These facts
have no signs
And these signs
point everywhere

The door opened.
The hogs ran outside.
The boys came back.
The big dog had the
  little dog in its mouth.
The dogs came back inside.
The big dog spit the little
  dog out.
The little dog could speak.

When an *e* is added
to *goed,* the *d* is
pronounced as a
Dutch *j* which is
sort of like an
English *y.*

How come?

Weet ik veel?
How do I know?

The high school dropout

rate in Baltimore is 50%.

disarray and poverty

glamour and energy

A whirlwind a snowball a take off

a Great Barbecue

Can you tell me
when White House press secretary
Marlin Fitzwater said that
"the forces of repression,
suppression and anarchy
cannot be allowed to continue"
was he referring to the
White House?

Tick-tock,
look at the clock.
Go now,
"to be there
where it is."

Oregon and Texas
are yet unsung

look outside

It's Amsterdam!

42

There's a canal in my eye.

so many faith
museums
each one of them
in their silence and emptiness
thriving

let's get together
and express our
"holy anger"

We make the weapons
with which you enslave us.

The new system.

We pay the taxes
with which you imprison us.

The new system.

In the textile industry
70% lost their jobs.
In the colleges
30% lost their jobs.
So you see,
they are doing very well
in the new system.

This is a necessity
we just have to accept.

If you saw images of
Christ everyday, how could you
not believe in Christ?

And now—

how can anyone
not believe in buying
and selling?

A student from Dresden:

"Now there are fewer friendships,
but more interests. Money, cars,
people without power.
A candle going out.
Our revolution dying."

Curious,
even the photographs we took
turned out very dark.

We have three windows
that overlook a canal.
Everything has worked
out well.

all talk there, wherever uttered,
having the pitch of a call

across the water

James put to another
direction

which will be heard?

memory

round and circular
it remains
after all else
it pulls back in
and remains

round and circular

memory

Questions become exclamations
America, a remembered Europe

The glasswort community turns
into a salt-marsh grass community.

L.A. into Den Hague

Rubles into Deutsche marks

X into Y

 and Z

back into the land

Remarkable: both
spoonbill and eider

breed here in the same area.

Sometimes their nests are in fact
within the same square meter.

Well, screw my face up
and push my glasses down

it's a wire from Fitzwater.
This time: "without fear
of infamy."

Paring knife

"Justice will prevail"

—President George Bush

Executive order
from two to seven days
—Governor Pete Wilson

Armor-plated kindness

that piece of the pie
too small to either
stand or stamp upon

without destroying your toes.

smoked meat
flesh
the sign meant
fresh
luxury
new vice
either way

accompanied
            after Herbert

a company
a compact

a compass
missing

i.e. the famous "Three Acorns"

The roadside was littered
with inspiration.

The poem
was one way to curb it.

Did you know that
the same year
Stevens
died Dickinson's *Collected
Poems* were published
for the first time and
the McDonald's Corporation
began?

Why, why are you
telling us this?
Shouldn't we be
discussing new ideas
of order?

In order to have a message
is it necessary to have an answer?
Why not just a question?
Accidents are more interesting
than accuracies.
To say—briefly—something
somewhere. An invitation
more than anything else here.

In his poem "Resignation"
Longfellow calls life on Earth
"a suburb of the life elysian."

There is no need to go
beyond America to find
alternatives to America.

I'm trying to stand in
it not for or against it.

One page to be filled
and be held accountable
for it.

It's the last time we're going to be
on the train past the new bridge in Rotterdam.

A view, an object,
or good food at a restaurant

Shakespeare and Cervantes
died in the same year

A walk along the dunes
west of Haarlem

Every morning the flagstones
were strewn with sand,
sometimes in patterns.

People get up to go
to the bathroom. I have already
gone. I was the first to go.
Again, I was the first.
What is next?

I haven't finished my wine
and already the coffee.

"Zonder suiker, alstublieft."

"Error, crime and adultery:
that's all that makes men
interesting."—Raymond Queneau

over Newfoundland
perhaps

"Error, crime, and adultery"

It Is Your Own

whirligig

on postcard front
verso:"Long live,"
the card ends.

Language lives.
"we can always do
what we do sometimes"
no, but what we do
all the time—attempt
a rending of the constant
yet inconsistent
asking

having
lived an unhappy life
the old man asked why
and by asking died
fulfilled, content in the question
unanswered.

the trails are uncut
the paths unmarked
our trial then to cut
them

anxious
anguished

the only light is that within
find it
and then hear the verdict
the trial ends
as you will end it

you are the trail
the path, the axe
the mark

a puzzlement
break silence and tell,
withdrawn from the ordinary,
who speaks with whom
and to what end?
there is virtue in distance
do not accept it, question
journey toward silence broken
an occasion

and neither seeing either self
but for a moment each other
so they meet
not on the street
but in the market
shake hands
no question now of knowledge
only a gesture a word
an opening

A Poem For Daniel Davidson

    as out to the street
we moved
     more brought into the program

       with words and wording
       like "earthquake," "volcano," and
       "spit it all away."

(spat then
 in the street
 no spats on
 but sneakers
 fast
 when not hung
 on wires

uptown

every morning every one gets
everything all ready again for another
morning

Work
hard mourning it is
till death

and after?

on wires uptown
hang words like
"earthquake," "volcano,"
and "spit it all away"

slapped by all the tourists outside
who will be allowed inside the off white

walls that surround, that stretch
to the lights a world where light
comes from the ground up,
volcanic grates erupt warm air
into faces lost in snow covered tracks

impossible to say a discouraging word
I hate capitalism
(have you seen any good movies lately?

memory equals money
equals squirrels made
squires forget that

if memory is beauty
remembered (Goethe), what
is the origin of beauty
and what of pain?

honey can't be got
without hard money
—not Keats,
Sacramento

memory equals money
equals spit

toleration as prison as
poison the mall
closed at night

here I am
gas from the digestive
track of an elephant

there it is tear it down
and still there it is
without words

an artist whose work
has been created
(death)

there it is

(an account)

it is hardly everything
that is represented by space

the sad elephant
remembers / remembered

the first year it is a gift
the second year it is an expense

one taste
sends the cork through the hoop

returns to all that's taxing
with words and wording
like

He's still there
I know him
What happened here
There's the bed he slept in
He still remains
Look close. The indentation
will be there for a month
or two

with words like "earthquake"
and "volcano"

he wrote in the first line of a foreword:

none of us knew the same thing at the same time

here I am

and wears its conscience on its sleeve

"spit it all away"

We describe these conventions
as benevolent; experience as one
long tracking shot

(to the edge / to the end

We thought
these bodies would
outlast
the years to come.

Now
we see that
the years to come
will outlast these
bodies.

Fortunes
All movements must be
motivated (or must be made
to appear so).

Now we see that

the passage of time is nothing to be
ecstatic about. Print books
on acid free paper; shred
after sixty days. Please
work with what's here.

What does it matter that blue
jeans were unknown to Cotton Mather?

"spit it all away

slate

What does it mean that
all the poetry sounds like prose
or like a pose?

clean slate

caution: wavy carpet

My mother was in the movies
the younger man said to the older
man when the latter returned.

You might recall her name.

The Constant

for David Bromige

Only the machine comes round, an anchor pulled through snow by a hay ball. Go to sleep and the tune awakes. But then there was too much talking down the hall until they all started in on the Lord's Prayer. In the night we could walk to town and back if the other fellow didn't change sides.

Their wings clash as cymbals do, but what of the whistle? Some of it is pretty; some, too loud. Ice forms a chair. No one will sit in it. There are no additional papers consulted on this subject. We take three steps uphill; one step down. While running through all this pageantry we could only think of the age old prescription for success: study hard or was it time equals money?

It is a popular melody. The panther leaps. The pier will be seventy feet wide, even if it is the first one. The flowers wilt on the floorboards of the car you drove to yesterday's picnic, but the car keeps going. It is as simple as that and that's that.

An act of will—to move the hand. Omit the fact: the erased body is its mind eased. As luck would have it, at just that moment the bell rang and we all heard the man singing softly in the long, dark distance. This must be our friend, a picture of evocation, poetry, the most beautiful bloom possible, the aesthetic idea that generates all that we need.

Surgery

She must decide on her philosophy before she operates on the pigeon that your basketball cut. The Waltons mobilize intriguing memories like the issue about when the people resist change. She must hypothesize what cup to save before she sews her shoes to the side of her car. The Waltons negotiate these intriguing ways as the recollections become the central issue as to why people like to resist change. She must ram this country into every college students' eyes (it's exam time) so that they may cut, saw, knife every sad store in the land. The Waltons like to resist change, to mobilize memories, to negotiate the way people recollect the central issue about why they did forget. It is the word that you can't see, she said, that will save you from all those looks that tie you to the car and The Waltons and the store and the failure to act.

The Medium

Slipped; then tried to get out.
"To where?"
To where there are trees
for symbolists to hang symbols upon.
Sink in the slits between the stones,
the words. Her
words. Her legs.
Her...

Language,
a household that wants introductions.
A man lands on shore. Which one?
This one beginning, "Will was no more."
Know what thing this is: the light.
Pink: an orb of radiant light.
Ridiculous to deliver rules to
or from. This
is only to prevent the effusions of
human blood. Thought, the reformation,
went on within newly constructed shadows
of wings. The House of Angles or
The Bowerbird Builds a Bower with which
to Attact and Woo its Mate.

Will no more was a mad prank after loss,
but circularity without precision. Habit
perhaps. The rain catches us
indoors on the floor.
Radiant at the window you
look out upon banners in the sky,
banners hung from where devils dance
in circles that enclose us.

Live with me in this world without being
of it. Clapboards cover

clay walls. Watch us as we watch what
is set before us. See
it offer a better story than this I
off you saying, "watch."

Each day becomes all days;
the middle of a web—its brightest light.

Order eliminates. The wall,
clay wall clapboards covered is
shadowed by
indistinct shapes of gray,
but there, there *see* that bright white spot!
There, us. (*Holding.*)

The ongoing
goes
on. It belongs beyond us.
An old garlic clove. What use
a tiny shoot? Three
green shoots now from one buried mass of
whiteness sending gray beard roots down;
dirt to one side. Healthy. No
fruit flies. Pangs
of joy was it /
angst shot through us? Smoke
it. A cure. A bridge

    to cross at night our dreams

a light gained in the crossing.

   Radiant!

We tied the third to rules and beat her
with the sequence of words, not the words themselves.
Rhythm is meaning if rhythm makes meaning understood.
No best word when all words are best.

(Is "better" better here?) *If you are attentive.*
What colors did they fly?

Adjectives limit the noun.

Near edges there are no sounds. Tongues
swing further from fruit. No white-pine
nor white-tail deer. Cannot sleep here.
Says is afraid and soon should die. We
wrapt her in our musicale warm in the
ornaments of sound. Sound we tied to
sense so much so that sight was mere vehicle
to get pleasing sound that need not have
made any sense. Neat edges, there are no sounds.

A gift of a silver pencil case is a necessity
for progress in French—the language of society.
Tonight we shall learn it & tomorrow to the Ball.
We step on the rim of God's robes—
the universe—with each syllable a slur.
Italian is for love, musical vowels, he would
speak it to his mistress, who has one, softly
almost whispering breath "la la forza del destino"
an empress easily impressed. Tied to sound,
we'll make soft sound hard and screw her
with it. Both of us at once. The ornamental is
occasionally useful.

I begged her to stop.
I said no not me but she kept on the feminine
past participle to break the will of the other,
that third not of us—a radish
planted in stone free soil early
spring to early summer and again in late
summer a radish she said *I*
looked like one
                    alchemical orb
          holding radiant light

60

from whence came
the wave into this dayglow room
a strobe repeating "biological objects
come in pairs," dear write
Vis, Force
Amnis, River
Cor, Heart
Artus, Joint
Filia, Daughter
Vis Amnis Cor Artus Filia
words picked
or sawed in half
constructed wonder constructs
pain like a plant's pushing through the earth
prefers the U-turn, no me—
back around and into
earth

The Certainties

Wound balls in a fist-size
head of ice burst the cardboard
quiet of two pit-bull eyes.
All tightens until after the all
quiet strikes. Human nature
must cornucopiate, a pendulum
swings less to sweet than to sweat.
Distance defeats. Memory loops
out of ice or presence loses
its ghost partner again. Alarms
bury light casualties, numerals
tongue the round lock.

And Who Conquers Servants BEHOLD Death

Dead and All repent throw time to eat food,
　　Strike churches slander know who conquers spirits;
　　Who searches remains awake to the call
Days are stars morning Dead things.
Stand so that great thunder is Come to slay
　　You loud-mouthed Elder now hear the worthy:
　　I saw Death opened for the sword blessing
And Death was followed with its other voice heard:
Honor the Lord with bowls golden full of earth
　　Wings of thy creatures and living wild beasts;
When a word Garments, comes so another black
　　Song for blood seals proclaiming—slain kill torch fire
By these plagues for he who sits trumpet—
　　Mankind, burning their mouths their endurance.

after Keats

The Obvious

It might be added but imply a sort of
    The one may be of Involved than in words
    Or likely in the pages such Transformation,
Sort of Obvious finding themselves in words
More general but a step from the passage,
    Of future meanings that for itself is—
    Words here we can note the sense it now can
Work from the words, a step but a considered—
We perhaps with that note and setting take
    A point, but not with fact, not with its pages
    Such as effect its sort of wholly fictive,
    Loose but as other sort of general and
Wit in the Finding of but certain words
    Lend to the fictive what is Obvious.

after Lang

Keep the Public

So God alive they will such as sense
   Brings will so long as not it may set out,
   The sense that People were not in any acts
   Thus did not increase, they served to show that
Some there inquired in China, the doorway
   Side streets shadow, the Word, critical fact;
   "But Did value priest-brothers, most feeling?"
   Due interest tenses. How Johnson, for culture
A system, most formal, "Mao this was war
   Dreamer came went by the name so. Who turned
   Mid book on death, mid book best known. When failed
This public: sometimes long hair beads path,
   Deaths were observed this crime itself history found;
   Act world my soul uncertain moves in ways."

after Milton

Lasting For Months Or Longer

Subfreezing temperatures in a twilit radioactive gloom.
Radioactive gloom in a twilit subfreezing temperatures.
In a twilit radioactive subfreezing temperatures gloom.
Radioactive gloom subfreezing temperatures in a twilit.
Temperatures radioactive gloom in a twilit subfreezing.
Gloom temperatures subfreezing twilit in a radioactive.
Subfreezing a temperatures in radioactive twilit gloom.
Twilit radioactive gloom temperatures in a subfreezing.
In gloom twilit a subfreezing radioactive temperatures.
Radioactive in a gloom temperatures twilit subfreezing.
A twilit gloom in radioactive subfreezing temperatures.
In a twilit radioactive subfreezing temperatures gloom.
Radioactive gloom in a twilit subfreezing temperatures.
Subfreezing temperatures in a twilit radioactive gloom.

September

You are not aware that night will scatter tokens along our paths.
You are not aware that this is a day that opens like a fan.
You are not aware that the clouds spin, brighten.
You are not aware that glittering rays hang amid blistered willows.
You are not aware that the earth hops lamely.

A crow escapes above the park: cutting, beating the air that it crosses.
It had paused momentarily at the ledge of the basin, at the ledge of the infinite.
The fountain trembles a deep, azure blue
while pigeons survey constellations of dahlias.
The wind that comes in from the west heats the asters.

after Robert Marteau

Vanished

All is well? That is not a difficult question. The horrible burden of this age blows you like a scarf that turns in the mud.

On the road to a palace, in the pit that you dig, in the mod emptiness of your room, you wake up. You ask for a window to the waves, to the stars, to the bird's wing, to the clock; to anything that whirls, to anyone who speaks. You ask what time is it and the window, the wave, the star, the bird, the clock answer: "Don't be a slave to the tortuous hands of this year, forget it: the skag, the poetry, the truth. Whatever, forget it. It is time."

after Charles Baudelaire

Two Infants Ago

I have seen your blue eyes of nineteen years
Give a pale thrill to thin sheets beneath
Elms, beneath tamarisks. I have seen your
Father grow tall about their elevations
High above his chest and your mother determine
Kisses for sweet jowls of alga.

In the conciliatory bower through which a false
Dawn reddens, I discover you like a rose
Upon the forest floor. My encampment is yours.
How clever your heat that quakes in shifts when
My heart burns. Dear child of the gutter,

How does nature view you who love your own
Childlike ways? Your beauty, such luster,
Enters and passes through every camp.
Yet, the moon will never be fully yours
While your hand encircles what love demands.

after René Char

Law and Order

There is too much snow!
These occasions are too dear
for postcards.

Some prefer the flame,
the flame and the wind
without a cloud in the sky

(the antitoxin, the sour
expense of judgment),
glossed over eyes, broken fingers

to the prudent snail of gametes.

after Francis Ponge

Tonsured

Bend over as light goes awry and
Laughter will kick backsides, words will fire
Indignation. The heat of less than beautiful
Storms breaks all the time—swatted,
Sunken and stolen—only to return
Later in a shower of fungus.
No need for a wall of words to enlist the truth,
Nor the scroll of the sea to anoint brave kings,
Nor feverish hands to encircle shafts
That levity, that perspicuity steer to slaughter
A forest where bowels, too, get the hatchet,
Where words flash in the darkness.
Enough: suppress the volcano. Whimper, struggle
And weep; then reject expunged acts. Dynamite
Always attracts itself; sound outstretches itself.
Nothing ever changes. The illumination of this
Opacity, this inferno embraces anguish.
Do not speak in order to sing.

after René Char

Siren Song

Keep away from the clock
    That tongues then bites
Keep away from the clock
    It is the gown of death

The revolving needle
    Sews up your worry
The revolving needle
    Sews up your ennui

Beyond every strong, handsome face
    Smiling in ignorance
Beyond every strong, handsome face
    Is embroidered despair

Keep away from the clock
    That tongues then bites
Keep away from the clock
    It is the gown of death

after Raymond Queneau

Pins and Needles

The pins and needles of eighteen meters
With hats on their tips,
They don't exist, they don't exist.

The pins and needles drag out a chair
Full of auks and ducks,
It doesn't exist, it doesn't exist.

The pins and needles speak English,
Speak Latin and Balinese,
They don't exist, they don't exist.
    Well! Why not?

after Robert Desnos

The Art of Poetry

Plucked out of the night were the eyes.
Tied up and withered were the hands.
A fever has been cured. A heart has been
Told to be a heart. A thundering demon
In the veins has vanished and a bleeding,
Dying mouth has been cleansed. Its voice
Reborn.

after Yves Bonnefoy

74

Stop Sign

The wind,
      across this dry heap of summer, frees
      us on its wave.
               The day is all sky.

Between several breaks, the land exacts itself. The
land sits status quo during puffs
that strip us.

Now on this sad, unmovable globe we have nearly
climbed the walls. That pit of day is ahead of us
again. That burning surface of the earth. The end
and the skin of our teeth
               leveled by those same puffs,
that frigid.

I recreate myself at the base of the facade
like the sad song of field hands.
               Nothing can extinguish my dance.

after André du Bouchet

A Few Sonnets More

Don't lose sleep, it'll come! You'll get closer,
you'll get warmer! More than the first word,
that which ends the poem brings death closer
and yet death heeds none of your words.

Don't think that it will wear off beneath the trees
or grant you one last breath while you finish writing.
Even if you drink from the mouth that quenches
the worst thirst, those wet lips with their sweet cry,

even if you grip madly the snarled rope
that your four arms make so that neither can creep
away from the burning dark of your sex,

it arrives, God knows by what route, to you both.
Far off or already here, don't lose sleep,
it arrives. One word to the next, you grow obsolete.

after Philippe Jaccottet

Dregs Pulled From Amnesia

memory of night
the gutter of metalanguages
black spots between obelisks

here is the silent train
and its procession of stag beetles
a hybrid charlot
weaves fixity there

after Guy Marchamps

Proffer

& those who neither professed
nor practiced any religion
write without language
Death Is A Chest of Bounty!
I am a jewel.

"some reckon"

Annihilation.

survivors dispute
"What you really need
Silence
is better than repetition
that gives way to greed.
to write acceptance
everything in the great
machine inclines to its
center

cast water into the center
cast water into the fire of contention
a river of swift water
body in contention incline to center
cast water into its center
cast water into the fire of contention

The weak enslave themselves and
we are weak.

strike the water
drumbeats
the water stained
with sun-tan oils,
mirror-like in the sun,

blackened by night.
Night into water,
fire into water
all these roads walks paths
all these ways

"some reckon"

Oedipus rests;
some other fellow
walks.

Again

a tapestry
like the page
so too the person
doesn't know how
all knowledge
wants out of fire,
wind, a sifting
marriage of two years
nor the library
passive again
from walking to listening
radiant before in
town uproar
no change
dead and already
plundered, a rug
a rope
there is no division
fulfilling the recurrent
music
look around
fan the flames
as here, jagged
pretend the boundaries
can be what precedes
rising again
out of the stream
that the water is
still pouring
high particulars
and accidents
interpreted as
authentic dog
pulling together
incessant sterility

carefully composed
in epic lusts
repeated
no matter what
shark explained
the tapestry
looked up
a wheel
worth expresses
tribute even here
an eagle
autobiographical (list
how to begin
bird like
the seed is also
social decay
light limits
which use of the word
at the very start
question by answer
this is what matters
labor leader pause
like the poem done
all throughout
mountain to atom
not a gathering
precisely
now this is all
gulf contingent
the wave
hoax, he said
release the flood
fan the fire
cumbersome
the page like the tomb
so persistent

Drums

The Cup
What holds the air of any expression?
Emptied, it says the following to me
on Wednesday: you are full of it.

White Paper
Lines man! He said. Like, they are
horizontal. I hear you. So what
will become of the paper? Eat it.

The Rug
"The Murders in the Rue Morgue." Not
there, but the spilt blood of those murdered
texts lapped in ceaseless waves at my feet.

Watch
What you hear is the flux of tense:
is/was, are/were, etc. Well, how about
it? What tense are you: then/now?

Wood Door
Pulled tooth. My floor has blood and
blood has sharp edges. It's like this: finished
when the right hand has the left hand tied.

The Clock
Smile. Your face moves me from point
A to point B. I've tried to stop you/
me, but I only bumped crudely into myself.

Stone Hallway

This house has sky to frame its every branch,
all that pattern held in just so. This
has been the story of rivers, oceans, and fenders.

Dennis Barone is a Professor of English at Saint Joseph College in West Hartford, Connecticut. He is the author of three recent books of fiction: *Abusing the Telephone* (Drogue Press, 1994), *The Returns* (Sun & Moon Press, 1996), and *Echoes* (Potes & Poets Press, 1997), which won the *America Award for Fiction*. His novella, *North Arrow*, is forthcoming from Sun & Moon. He is co-editor with Peter Ganick of the noted anthology *The Art of Practice: Forty-Five Contemporary Poets* (Potes & Poets Press, 1994) and he is editor of *Beyond the Red Notebook: Essays on Paul Auster* (University of Pennsylvania Press, 1995). His essays on early and contemporary American literature have appeared in journals such as *American Studies, Critique, Proceedings of the American Philosophical Society*, and the *Review of Contemporary Fiction*. A graduate of Bard College, he received his Ph.D. in American Civilization from the University of Pennsylvania in 1984, and in 1992 he held the Thomas Jefferson Chair, a distinguished Fulbright lecturing award, in the Netherlands.